THE
SEX
CONTRACT

The Manual That Teaches Couples
How to Establish Their Own Sex Contract
While Empowering Each Other
to Fall in Love Again

P AND J LEE

authorHOUSE®

AuthorHouse™
1663 Liberty Drive
Bloomington, IN 47403
www.authorhouse.com
Phone: 833-262-8899

Published by AuthorHouse 03/29/2022

ISBN: 978-1-6655-5624-8 (sc)
ISBN: 978-1-6655-5623-1 (e)

Library of Congress Control Number: 2022905952

Print information available on the last page.

*Any people depicted in stock imagery provided by Getty Images are models,
and such images are being used for illustrative purposes only.
Certain stock imagery* © *Getty Images.*

This book is printed on acid-free paper.

Disclaimer

This book contains true experiences and is only intended for readers over the age of eighteen. The stories shared in this book are the real-life accounts of a stripper from her and her husband's perspectives. We are not trained therapists or professional counselors. This book is about providing couples with the tools to be transparent and honest about their most intimate needs and desires. *The Sex Contract* is intended to help open-minded couples meet each other needs in a structured and progressive manner. This manual was written for couples who desire the empowerment of having the best relationship possible.

Contents

Introduction

Namaste everyone. My name is P. Lee. I am a fifty-one-year-old Caucasian female. I'm married to a sexy fifty-three-year-old Islander named Jay. Jay and I decided to coauthor this book to empower other couples to live their best lives, both in and out of the bedroom. In my opinion, over thirty-three years of marriage and my employment as a topless exotic dancer has provided me with the experiences needed to write this book and grant couples with the innate tools to better their relationships. My husband and I were merely optimistic kids in love when we got married in 1988. I was eighteen, and my husband was twenty. We have been together since, not without our ups and downs. During our marriage, I earned my Associate's and Bachelor of Science degrees in nursing. We have created two sons and one grandson, and they are the center of our world.

I was born in the Midwest to a single mother. I didn't meet my biological father until I was thirty-nine years old. According to my mother, my biological father was a married man that had sexually assaulted her when she was sixteen years old. While pregnant with me, my mother found out that my biological father's wife was also pregnant. It was obvious that my bio-dad had a type—both women were redheads. By the time I was six months old, my mom had already been married twice, and neither man was my father. Unfortunately, my stepdad was aware of my bio-dad. Both my father and stepfather lived in the same city and were always hostile toward one another. They had a turbulent history and were longtime competitors for my mother's love. They would often get into bar fights with one another, make rude comments at the other's expense, and exchange dirty looks when they were out in public.

My stepfather often took any opportunity to exact his revenge on my biological father by being physically, sexually, and verbally abusive toward me. For example, when I was seven years old, my stepfather would watch me take baths through a small hole in our bathroom wall. That lasted a couple of months until my mother had the wall repaired. Shortly after that, when my mother would go to bingo, he would ask me to take my underwear off, sit on his back, and massage him. That moment skewed how I viewed men. I thought it was so strange that a father would ask his daughter to do these sick acts. I had no idea that he wasn't my biological father. None! From a young age, I learned that men are very primal. They would do anything to address their sexual needs, even with a child. My stepfather was a sadistic individual, and the thought of what he did still sickens me to this day. However, I personally consider myself lucky—he never physically touched me. Those interactions with my stepfather inevitably left me with a negative opinion of men because I truly believed that all men were the same.

The reason I brought up my childhood drama is to reinforce how important it is to address the sexual needs and desires in your personal relationship to prevent unwanted advances toward your children. I know that's hard to hear, but it's an unfortunate reality. When I turned thirteen, one of the most impactful days of my life took place—my mother and stepfather divorced, and my mother and I moved into our own home.

During their divorce proceedings, I learned that my stepfather was not my biological father while discussing child support. He didn't want to pay my mother child support. For the first thirteen years of my life, my mother led me to believe that my father was a sexual predator. Her actions had a detrimental impact on my life, making it difficult to trust people I interacted with and loved. Eventually, my mother lost custody of me, and I was forced to live with my maternal grandparents. I loved them both immensely, but even they couldn't corral the rage in my mind and heart or the distrust in my soul.

Two months after I turned eighteen, I met my husband through a mutual friend. From the moment I laid my eyes on him, I believed that he was the tallest and most handsome man I had ever seen. He even had a sexy accent. He was so kind, patient, and loving. Unlike most men I had met, he was not a player or a guy who took advantage of women. He was straight from the islands and untainted. For me, it was love at first sight. He was a gift sent to me from the maker of the universe to make up for all that I had been through. When we met, I was just leaving high school, and he was serving in the military. At the time, I didn't have a real job, so I made the personal decision to capitalize on my boobs and work at the local strip club. We were young and naive, full of passion and determination, and in need of financial stability. My job at the strip club allowed us to make ends meet while I took college courses to become a registered nurse. I feel like my experiences as a stripper have given me firsthand knowledge of the male species. This knowledge was invaluable in helping me better my own marriage and eventually, in writing this book. I hope that you enjoy it.

1

My Message

My message is pure and comes from a place of experience, love, honesty, and integrity. It's as simple as being open, honest, and transparent about your needs. You want that partner to compliment, compensate, cherish, and complete you. You should do the same for them. You want your partner to inspire you to be the best version of yourself, and in turn, you do the same for them. Encourage your partner to be the healthiest version of themselves and show by example. Relish every second that you have with your partner, as life is too short. Do not waste time on petty stuff that robs you of quality time with your partner. Instead, make love and become one with your partner on every level. Your love can inspire you to accomplish everything from your life goals to be the best role model to your children and everyone you encounter.

Make love to your partner as often as you can. Your sexual healing is the action that connects you with your partner on such a deep level that no one can come between. Don't let your insecurities come between you and your partner. Learn to love yourself and be confident in your own skin. Give yourself to your partner. Tell your partner what you need and be able to receive their needs with loving energy. If you love your man and want to keep him, then show him he is of the highest priority. Let your man know that he is your King Kong in bed. He needs validation just as you do. It is of the utmost importance to meet the sexual needs of your relationship unless you have a health condition that prevents it. (In that case, you should talk with professionals on ways to address the sexual needs of your relationship.) Having regular intercourse or some type of release is a must. We need to view sex the same way as brushing and flossing our teeth every day. It must be a conscious decision. We must not only brush but also floss to preserve our teeth's foundation: our gums. It's the same concept as being married and servicing your partner's needs—protect the foundation of your relationship by having consistent sex. Men need to feel connected and being intimate with one will show him that he is the priority.

What I call the "sex contract" is of the utmost importance in your marriage and comes second only to raising and being good role models to your children. *Sex* should be an occurring event in your home. We should all have a sex contract established. It does not have to be written down, just understood between the couple. Again, I'm not a therapist, but I'm speaking as a former stripper who has been married to the same man for over thirty-three years. I attribute my long marriage to the advice that I am openly sharing with you. I believe that when we orgasm or ejaculate on the regulated basis of the sex contract, we are all happier and less anxious people who will ultimately deal with stress better. We would all be the best versions of ourselves and amazing role models. Everyone should have a sex contract, but each sex contract should be unique and different.

Jay: My simple message is this: enjoy every single day like it's your last day. For every negative issue you have in life, there is a way out of it that doesn't require you to lose precious time. I know it's easy to say that now, but I sure wish I'd had that mindset as a young, immature person. Explore all the possibilities that make you and your significant other happy, and that's all that matters. I always tell my wife that until those other people in your life—including friends and family—pay your bills and assist you in living life, they shouldn't matter other than saying hello and goodbye.

2

Confessions of a Stripper

Before we get into what a sex contract is, we need to discuss some of the experiences that lead up to it. Without my experiences as a stripper, I would never have been able to write this book. Working in the strip club allowed me to observe firsthand how primates act around gorgeous women and alcohol. Stripping allowed me to elevate my life and career because it was a steppingstone to a better life. My husband understands that if I wasn't in love with him, my significant other would be a cool seventy-five-year-old sugar daddy who owns a plane.

I would never choose money over the butterflies I still get when I see my man. I love and need him. I want him to always love and need me. That is why I try to keep my stripper game up, even at my age. I eat right, exercise, and continue to use my home stripper pole. I have a pair of clear stilettos that always sit next to it, just waiting for me to play some R & B and go with the music. That's it—that's all you must do. The money I made while dancing allowed me to provide self-care for my family and myself. We went on cruises and enjoyed life. My husband

and I were able to get regular massages and spend our time as we pleased instead of pushing a timecard.

I started dancing at the age of seventeen in a military club. At that time, we were only allowed to dance in swimsuits or negligees. I danced half a dozen more times at the age of eighteen, but I didn't really get into dancing until I was thirty. I know that seems old, but I looked twenty-something. I was making more money than any of the twenty-year-olds without having to take my panties off and show the vagina. I was older, more refined, and played the long game. I had long, spirally blonde hair with a dark tan and deep blue eyes with eyelashes that looked like spiders' legs. I was hot, confident, and completely supported by my husband, who counted my take every night. It was thrilling to make so much money and learn so many things about men.

Men are predictable, for the most part, as they all need validation and attention. They need to feel like they are kings. Men need to feel good about themselves, and there are few better places for stroking the male ego than the strip club. Strip clubs create an atmosphere where women dominate the playing field. Women sit back in the dressing rooms, applying lotion and makeup. They transform themselves into gorgeous, perfumed, sexual beasts that slay men and take their money. Men eat it up and spend and spend to compete for the attention of the stripper—for the smell and touch of a beautiful woman and the illusion of being her man. You would never even know that many of these men are married.

Strippers will sometimes caress the back of a man's neck and hold his hand, creating the façade of courtship and a connection that alludes to what could happen next. Many strippers, including me, would massage men's necks and shoulders as if they were kings. You would have thought those men had never been touched like that. Men are like clay around gorgeous women. I always loved bringing my man to the club to watch me and see the other women dance. I loved dancing for other men in front of him so that he knew what he had. It was erotic, and I loved it, not to mention what it did for our sex life. The experiences that my husband and I gained were supremely exciting. I was dancing at three of Hawaii's top clubs. I loved everything about working in the club, except the cigarette smoke.

I started dancing when I was taking my prerequisite courses for the nursing program. I hated working as a phlebotomist for ten dollars an hour, waking up at five in the morning, and having to give most of my paycheck to childcare. I guess I saw topless dancing as a steppingstone—I mean, stripping pays a lot more than nursing, but it was always a short-term plan for me. I was using one hustle for the next. Even though Hawaii allowed nude dancing, I only took my top off. I figured it was just tits. My vagina was for my husband. I would make anywhere from $500 to $3,000 a night without ever showing my "downstairs." So why not? I learned so many things about men and women while working at the club. I made my money because of my looks, and the idealization of making love to me kept them coming back. I often told them what I would do if they were my men.

I also never took off my wedding ring. I told my clients that my husband and I were separated but that I would never disrespect my marriage—I believed in marriage, and if I were to marry again, it would be the same thing. Those men offered to pay my bills and take me on lavish trips, as I was a separated stripper with a Southern accent and worthy of taking home to Mama—and in nursing school. I let my clients know never to disrespect me or ask questions they wouldn't want to be asked about them in the same situation. Those men learned quickly that if they were worthy of me, they would never push that. Only a few did, and they were replaced with ten more who wouldn't that same night. I also told them that they would never trust me if I cheated on my husband. They all fell for it because after they thought about it, they knew it was true. They kept coming back for the chase, the anticipation, and the fantasy. Also, for validation and the strategic attention that they received.

We all need validation at some point in our lives. I always validated my clients. They felt like sexy beasts around me. I knew exactly what to say. I had no problem making dietary recommendations and encouraging them to keep the CrossFit up, even knowing damn well that they had not set foot in the gym in years. A stripper will make a man feel like he is King Kong. He could be the fattest guy, but that stripper will make him feel like he's the fittest. He will be in the gym the next week, getting fit because now he feels good about himself. Men need attention in addition to sex—not too much but quality attention. When I was in the club, I acted like a lady, and then on stage, I ground my body to show them what could happen if I were on top.

It's all an illusion and fantasy. The music totally adds to the mix and creates just the right atmosphere for men to think they are gods. Many of the men that come to the strip club get some ethanol in them, forget that they are married, and make fools out of themselves. The strippers are there to capitalize and play head games that lure these guys in. It's about the attention the men get. Sex is important, but attention is what they're seeking. I played the long game, meaning I wanted rich clients. It was more about integrity, and these men thought that they might be "the guy."

I made them think that I was just waiting to see how things panned out with my separation. I told them that they had so much potential and made me feel like a princess. It was too easy—and sometimes hard—to keep it going. I was almost able to have a double life. I never had sex with any of my clients, but sometimes emotions were involved. I felt flattered but had no other love feelings for those men. Of course, I loved the jewelry, money, and gifts. If not for me, then all those things would have been for someone else. I decided it should be me. For the most part, playing with men's emotions was a game. If they were in the club, they were fair game. I never felt sorry for the married guys. Some of the men didn't cheat. They were there for a little look and variety, and those were cool in my book. The men who didn't cheat were an exceedingly small percentage compared to the ones that did. Some men go to the club looking for a wife, and it is not a game to them at all. I could see why men fall in love with strippers and vice versa.

There were a few instances I felt bad about. The guy that made me feel truly awful was a nineteen-year-old that we will call CJ. I had just turned thirty, and he fell fast and hard. He told me that he'd had sex about a dozen times. Half of those times were overseas, as he was in the navy. CJ proposed to me and asked about having children. All I had to do was say the word, and his family would take care of any fees related to my divorce and travel to the mainland from Hawaii. He had it all planned out based on a facade. He came from a rich family and only joined the military because of a fight with his stepdad. He was an amazing man but not my man. He knew I was married, and he pursued me anyway.

We did have a small kiss during a private dance. I'd had too much Cristal. It wasn't planned. It just happened while I was dancing. Before that, the most I had ever done was allow him to smell the Victoria's Secret in my hair, or I would squeeze the side of his leg and run my hand against his downstairs, over his pants. That was the extent. I was making at least $500 per hour; it was all good. CJ told me that the thought of having sex with me was better than the best sex he'd ever had. He wanted to sweep me off my feet and take care of my children. Many of the guys from overseas fell in love within days of coming into the clubs. They would go back for a private dance and come out in love. I saw so many people having sex in the back during a private dance. I would see strippers doing everything you could imagine—sometimes tricks. It was awful, but that was their lives and the reality of club life. I only lightly ground on certain men (like CJ) during private dances. No touching was allowed. Only the strippers were allowed to touch. Strip clubs are dirty places, no matter how nice they look.

Smart strippers will establish boundaries and hold to them. They won't give in to sex or drugs. A little weed or champagne is OK, but no hard drugs. Smart strippers will keep themselves up on every level. They need to look so good that men are tripping over each other to get to them. Once they do, the strippers will make those men feel like the sexiest beings on the planet. It works almost every time. Strippers will give them unimaginable attention. Strippers make their money by giving men the attention they are not getting at home. It doesn't matter whether their partners are giving them attention; it wasn't enough because they still made it to the club.

Private dances are expensive, and they are the fastest way to make the most amount of money. In addition, expensive drinks range from twenty to fifty dollars. Champagne is even higher. I would get both at the same time. The guys would pay because that kept me with them. Once a Japanese psychiatrist ordered a bottle of Cristal for me and asked me not to get on the stage.

That night, he wrote a check for $4000 and hired me as his personal assistant and office manager. All because of my strip club experiences. Many of the things that you have heard or read about strip clubs are true—and then some. Many strippers get stuck in the club because of drugs or alcohol. If they aren't saving, investing, or going to school, they have no chance of taking their lives to the next level of financial security.

As a stripper, you learn to read men and become whatever woman they need in that moment. Within ten minutes of conversing, a stripper can learn more about your man than you ever will. This is a true statement. Do you think he will share how he lusted after the girl at work or how his cock got hard for his first love? Hell no, he won't. But he will tell the stripper. Men usually need to explain how they are overworked, financially stress, not treated right, etc. They get very resentful when they aren't sexually satisfied. This resentment has exacerbated the longer they must wait. When other problems get thrown into that mix, nothing good can come. The beauty is that all of this can be prevented by giving your husband the attention he needs. Don't force him to go to the club with naked women and alcohol, unless you plan to go with him. When your man is in the strip club, he will have the confidence to express his thoughts, especially after a few drinks. Many strippers capitalize on that and empathize, providing great comfort to men. That's when you run the chance of losing your man. Strippers and other women will provide the attention that your man thinks he's not getting at home. Some strippers will take away all that you have worked for just because they gave your man attention. Of course, the stripper is lying most of the time. But your man will still believe it. He needs to be the king of the narrative.

I used to make men feel like the only man on the planet. I massaged their necks while looking into their eyes; covering their face with my long, blond hair; and making them think they were the sexiest men in the world. In that moment, they were. I was extremely convincing and told them that I couldn't stop thinking of them. I made them think that they were the biggest, strongest men on the planet and that I always felt so safe. They continued to spend their money, and I continued to stroke their egos, massaging their necks without ever compromising myself. Even though they were frustrated, they continued to come back and pay me. I was the kind of woman that they could take home to mama but also make that money. I was a nursing student to them and always had my schoolbooks on the table. They loved that even more. Those men knew I was not a typical stripper. I was on a different path, and they wanted to be on it with me. I was a beast with a plan for my family, which they funded. Strippers make their money by providing attention to their clients. I always told my clients that they looked like they worked out frequently. It was all a game, and they fell for it 99 percent of the time.

Men will eventually get upset and show their emotions, another mistake that a stripper can use against them. Some of the military men's wives would get fat and or were too controlling. These men would go to the club and find a fit, sexy stripper that met his needs. Or we would hear about military men that went overseas and left their controlling wives for submissive women from other countries. In some countries, women are raised to please their men. Or to please your man. That is when you take control of your relationship. You can be the exception if you put in the work to ensure your spouses' needs are met so they won't venture into strip clubs.

Make sure your man is the one you want to be with. Love him enough, to be honest, and transparent. Meet his needs in a nonjudgmental atmosphere. Let him know that he is your king, and you want to please him. The one common denominator in the strip club was the attention men received. Give your man the attention he needs. And above all else, don't restrict your man from going to the club if that's what he wants to do. Go with him, or he will go to the club behind your back. You don't want to be in a relationship where you feel like he is doing something behind your back. You certainly do not want to come across as a parental figure, making your partner want to avoid you as much as possible. Figure out what it is that you have a problem with and address it. Strip clubs aren't only for men. Women often have a great time when they go. Work on channeling your inner stripper. Dress sexier and apply makeup more often. Pull out those negligees and make them part of your normal attire. Go with him. Embrace other beautiful women. Variety and youth are always nice to look at. Trust me, there is nothing wrong with admiring the beauty of another woman, especially when done with your husband. Now if your partner is a pervert, that's another story. Going to strip clubs and other activities can be addressed in your sex contract.

I'm not trying to stereotype everyone, but most people will cheat in the right situation and for many different reasons. I am confident that you can prevent it by establishing and sticking to the expectations of your sex contract. Cheating won't happen on your watch if you execute your sex contract under your terms and stick to it. Embrace your inner stripper in the privacy of your home before heading out to the club. Put on your favorite jam and have your husband order some stilettos, negligees, lingerie, and sexy clothes for you. What a turn-on that will be for him. Let him know that you cannot wait to wear them for him. Strip for your partner. Let him know how much you love the way he feels inside you. Keep your partner out of the strip club unless you're with them or OK with letting him go alone. Establish some rules of engagement and address them in your sex contract. Be the sexiest version of yourself that you can be. Be sexier for your man and own it. Spend a few extra seconds applying your mascara. Make sure your lipstick is on point. Encourage your partner to go to the gym with you. Get in shape and become the best version of yourself. There is a stripper inside of every woman. Bring it out and let her free. Use your clouds of pheromones to make your point! Go to the strip club with your man.

Jay: When I first met my wife, she was working as a dancing girl at one of the military clubs on base. I didn't meet her at the club, but I was aware of her situation when she told me. I even escorted her a few times and watched, upon her request. I was a very conservative person, so this wasn't an ideal situation for me. But it wasn't a serious relationship at that point, so her job was none of my business. When she asked me to go, I was very hesitant at first, but I gave it a go anyway. It was a moment in life when I dropped my barrier and encountered something new.

The later times she stripped were purely for financial reasons. We were strained financially, and she was looking to make a career. Money was a big issue. I never looked at it any other way. I trusted her. I never saw her as just a stripper because away from the clubs, she was a devoted wife and mother. She was motivated to make a better life by pursuing educational opportunities and trying to make a career. She always reminded me that it was temporary. She would strip until we could get our financial issues under wrap.

Our financial strains were our pitfalls because we were young, naïve, and clueless as to how to manage them. Her stripping enabled me to understand what that profession entails. It wasn't always about sex. I met a few dancers who were in the same predicament as us. Heck, her best friend at that time was another dancer with a military guy. We hung out together. A few times, we all went to the same club and watched our significant others wow the crowd. It was crazy, but I was never jealous because I trusted my wife. She would divulge exactly what a person wanted or said. The only negative perspective I saw was her safety when she left the club late at night. There were plenty of nights when I would wake up in the early hours and she wasn't home. It worried me. It wasn't the cell phone age yet, so I was uneasy, wondering if she was OK.

3

Threesomes

Threesomes are the ultimate test of how your man will act when in the company of another woman. When we got married, my husband told me that he would love to have a threesome. At first, I was upset, thinking that I wasn't enough. Then, I realized that he was being honest with me about something he wanted to try. We were in our early to mid-twenties when we decided to partake in sexual acts with other women. The threesomes were usually my idea and for different reasons. The first reason was to get it out of the way. All of our friends were doing it. We were a young military couple, so we were around many different people who traveled the world. They would tell us stories of being in Italy and France, where threesomes were no big deal. Threesomes were a hot topic, so I'm sure some of you can relate. They always have been and always will be something people do. Please don't confuse what we did with swinging or any other activity that required other men or switching partners. My husband and I are not swingers; that isn't our thing. I have OCD, so I haven't partaken in any of the encounters other than inserting my finger and feeling their vaginas. That was a major turn-on for me.

To this day, I still get turned on when I think about what I witnessed in the privacy of my own home. I loved the way the women took charge of my husband. They had high standards of hygiene, so when my husband tasted them, they were clean. I knew this because I smelled my finger after inserting it into each of them. Of course, they all had baths first. It was science in the making. I got to touch, and my husband tasted. We experienced a triple connection. Those ladies had their needs met by a gorgeous islander with an accent. They all would have done it again. I'm glad my husband and I experienced other women because it reinforced our relationship. He was less curious about other vaginas. I'm also lucky that it didn't backfire. I had no way of knowing or predicting how my husband would act after the fact. Threesomes, in general, are not that big of a thing. They aren't something that we ever did again. However, we still use those experiences in our lovemaking to this day. Threesomes seem to be the norm in other countries like France and are becoming more and more acceptable in the United States. There are many nude establishments such as bathhouses, nude colonies, nude cruises, massage parlors, and hot springs. Sexuality is a beautiful thing and should be expressed respectfully.

My husband and I had threesomes on three separate occasions. My husband penetrated and orally stimulated the women while I watched. He never had an orgasm with any of the women. I know that's not normal, but it's true. My husband and I both feel that women are beautiful. We treated the women that we connected with very respectfully. While stripping in Hawaii, I was around sexy women from all over the world. Their youth, energy, and body movements turned me on. Women are amazing creatures, and I wanted my husband to experience different women the same way one would taste food—for the experience. Thinking about it is turning me on right now. One benefit of a threesome is that you can use those experiences throughout your marriage. I still bring up one experience at least a dozen times per year. I was twenty-five at the time. Our partner, Angie, was this sexy twenty-year-old was so tight, fit, and flawless. I loved watching my husband's penis, Pinky, go into her tight, pink vagina. He pulled out, and her tight pussy was covering Pinky with all that juice. It was such a turn-on. After she showered, my husband and I made love until we exploded. Because this was a true experience, we can still use it during intercourse to make our orgasms explosive. We didn't stay in contact with any of the women. I wish we had; I really do. This isn't to scare you. You don't want to chance the person you choose contacting you or your husband unless you are okay with that. Our partners are never going to be my husband's lovers or wives. They were just proxies, amazing tastes of variation.

Don't get me wrong, I love seeing Pinky inside of me. But I get to see that every day. Every now and then, I get an itch that must be scratched. I might want to go to the strip club and watch beautiful women with my man. In that case, we just go and enjoy. We love to tip the ladies, as that is how they make their money. Money is the motivator, and I'm not mad at those girls for using their bodies to make it. It sure beats slinging burgers for minimum wage.

I like to consider myself confident and open-minded. My husband trusts me because I speak my mind, and I'm open-minded enough not to get caught up in the small stuff. Because I live my life in a trusting environment, my spirit is always free. I never feel like a caged bird or like I'm missing out on something else. My husband gives me this fucking relentless security and trust, and I would never want to mess that up. I want to give him anything and everything he might want or need, whether he asks for it or not. He deserves it for all that he has given me. There were times in our marriage when he acted as my handler when I couldn't channel my anxiety. I could go on and on with more reasons why I want my husband to be treated like a king. He is my king. I love knowing that he has gotten to experience different things in life. My husband is an incredibly happy man—a fat cat if you will. He has the best of both worlds: a woman who loves him and a freak in the sheets. He never asked for any of the threesomes, nor does he want another one. But if he ever asked for a threesome, I would arrange it before he could even exhale. The knowledge that he can ask for one at any point is reassuring for him.

There was a point while I'm writing this, we were intimate almost every day during a three week stretch. That had nothing to do with another woman. My husband can't seem to get enough of me. I know he loves me and I am a lucky woman, still with the man I fell in love with at eighteen. I'm experiencing more passion than ever before. When we make love, it is so intense. He usually starts by kissing me, but on certain occasions, he will start at my toes. He will kiss and lick from my toes, up to my thighs; all around my fat, pink pussy; and all the way back down to my other foot. Then he will lick up to my nipples, nursing on both breasts evenly. Eventually, he will reach my tongue, kissing me. Then he'll go down my neck and back to my downstairs until I can no longer take it. At that point, we will flip around and perform sixty-nine. I'll bury his face in my vagina, almost suffocating him, but he won't struggle. I'll suck on Pinky as deeply as I can, gripping with both hands while deep throating him up and down. Sometimes it's difficult to deep throat his penis because Pinky is so huge and fat. I will suck on his balls while he sucks on my vagina, licking and teasing me. I'll continue to suck Pinky as deeply as I can, gently gripping his pulsating penis in my hands until he explodes. After we orgasm, we will hold each other to lock in a positive memory that will not only reinforce our bond but will also make us feel good.

We always lay together, listening to each other's hearts beat while sweaty. In that moment, I know what heaven must feel like. I am most vulnerable right after we have sex. I'm so emotionally and physically satisfied that all I want to do is be in the protection of my husband's huge chest. I need total love and transparency in that moment. Those are the moments when we openly talk and get closer. We are vulnerable together.

Holding my husband right after sex lets him know that nothing is more important to me than strengthening our bond. We reminisce about the old days and days to come. It's phenomenal, and we are learning that it only gets better with age. Please appreciate that I am sharing our deepest, darkest fantasies and most intimate moments. It took a lot to admit how turned on I was when I saw my husband penetrate another woman. I am confident that there are others like me that imagine their partners with other people.

This book is not to encourage you to have threesomes. It's to encourage you to be open, honest, and transparent about your needs. It's about opening your eyes to all the possibilities that you and your partner can explore. Set goals and boundaries. The rest is up to you. If your marriage is in trouble, you need to seek professional help immediately. Don't nag or force anything on your partner. Simply tell them that you love them and want to make it work. Let your partner know that you are present but give them space to prevent further damage to your relationship.

Sex doesn't fix everything, but in a loving relationship, it can knock out unnecessary tension that causes a magnitude of problems. I believe that when you have sex on a regular basis, it prevents many unnecessary fights. Sex and marriage go hand in hand. If one is lacking, the other will be also affected. Marriage is about safety, honesty, and being your most vulnerable self. Be willing to do just about anything for your relationship or marriage, whether that's performing different sexual acts, going back to school, or getting a job. Better your career so that you can support your family. Be a better example for your partner and children. Let them know how dedicated you are to your marriage and their wellbeing. You or your partner should buy a stripper pole and some stilettos. Use the pole for support, at your own risk, until you have mastered the art of it. If you are overweight, this is the time to get in shape. I'm not suggesting that you become some version of yourself that doesn't fit into your reality. I want you to feel good about yourself. Get your sexy on, but that doesn't mean you need to be a size two.

I wanted to share some of my intimate moments to assure you that your sex life should be your priority. It will only come second to caring for your children, especially as you get older. My husband and I felt that sharing our sex lives would inspire other couples to make their relationships the priority. Sex must be part of your routine. So be transparent and honest about your needs. Establishing a sex contract will change the trajectory of your relationship by preventing tension and resentment and decreasing the probability of your partner cheating. People are human, and their needs will be met one way or another. Address those needs on your own terms, as established in your sex contract. For me, sex is a medicine that optimizes my body. Everyone must take the time to ensure they have sexual connections with their partners. If your partner is out of town, you should masturbate. I recommend planning sexy activities to keep your relationship in check. Keep it fun and interesting. Don't become complacent. You could do small, inexpensive things like feeding your partner strawberries and whip cream, running a bath, or adding some flower petals.

Do not let your sex life turn into a job. Make it fun and let your partner know what your needs are. For example, lick whipped cream off a strawberry, and then give your partner some. Slowly take another berry and put it on the tip of your tongue. While your partner is taking a bath, lay on your back, spread your legs, and stick the strawberry inside your vagina or lay it on top of your penis and have her or him eat from there. Tell him to take it out because you need him inside of you. Grab those berries and get your antioxidants on. Ask him to nurse on your clit, suck your breasts slowly, and stick his finger up your ass (if that's what you like). Get in the bath with him and wash each other. Prepare for what's to come after your bath. Do not go right for his penis. Make him want it so bad he has blue balls. Lick his toes. Suck anywhere on his body, except his penis. Then suck on his balls, pulling his hair with your tongue. Slowly work your way down to his ass and stick your tongue deep in his asshole. Changing positions to get a better angle, spread his ass cheeks as far apart as possible without causing discomfort. Imagine that you are going down on another woman, but it's your partner's ass. Give him all the pleasure if that's something he's comfortable with. By the way, this can also work on any couple whether you are straight or gay. The same concept applies.

If you decide to bring other women or men into your relationship, it must be in a controlled environment of your choosing. Again, safety is your highest priority. Mentally and physically protect yourself while maintaining integrity and dignity. Not every person wants to have a threesome, but most people are curious. They like variety. I'm not saying married people should have hall passes. I'm just saying that you can prevent sexually transmitted diseases, stalkers, and crazy people from entering your sex life. And with all the apps they have these days, it's easier and easier to cheat than it ever has been. I don't want you to get cheated on or to put your health at risk. I am simply asking you to take control of your life and make it what you and your partner need it to be. Make it rock-solid by being honest and transparent. You don't have to have a threesome to be successful. It was a great experience for my husband and me. They added a level of excitement that only could have been achieved from a threesome. I just happen to be a freak, and my husband is an incredibly lucky guy.

Jay: Did I mention that I was a very conservative person? Yet here we are with another situation that challenges that point. Yes, the idea of being with two women sounds amazing, but it's also complicated. I agreed to this because, in my mind, my wife really wanted it for herself. It was something that never crossed my mind until she brought it up (numerous times). I was the agreeing party, so it wasn't all about her. I could have stuck to my guns and said no. In the end, it was our idea. The experiences made our marriage stronger. For a wife, seeing her husband licking and fucking another pussy in front of her and not killing him can be crazy and unimaginable. But my wife was more willing to test the waters. It turned her on. This showed me how much my wife loves me, and for that, I was willing to spend the rest of my life devoted to her every need. She still uses those memories to spice up our sexual activities. It was crazy to see those women agree to what my wife asked of them, but they were willing participants, even though they were all younger than we were. It was fun, but there were no attachments. It was always a one-and-done deal. The second girl said she wished that she had a relationship like ours and hearing that made me a happier husband.

4

The Sex Contract

My husband and I established our sex contract about five years ago, when we realized that we needed an intervention in our marriage due to unnecessary fighting. I was a traveling nurse and away a lot. We had phone and video sex, but it wasn't the same as penetration or human touch. We fought over stupid things, wasting our lives. We both knew that sex was the pinnacle of our relationship. Many people think that their marriage license is a contract in terms of sex. When we got married, we signed our marriage contract, but that differs from our sex contract.

A sex contract is an agreed plan to meet the sexual needs and expectations of a relationship. It is a verbal or written contract between two partners that are in a committed relationship. It is dependent on one thing: sex. You do not have to be married. The contract allows sex to be a constant in the bedroom, executed at the decided frequency. It can be modified at any time if both parties agree. By implementing a sex contract, couples will grow closer, make intimate connections, release pent-up tensions, and prevent unnecessary fights. However, sometimes life, drugs, alcohol, and other addictions prevent happy-ever-after endings. In those situations, we encourage you to seek professional counseling.

Some of the biggest problems in married life are sexual expectations and the resentments that follow when those expectations aren't met. Usually, men feel like they are being deprived. Sexual deprivation can lead to a lot of tension and stress, exacerbating the entire issue. Your partner may feel rejected and unwanted, and that's when outsiders are most likely to penetrate your relationship. Unfortunately, it took my husband and me many years before we instituted our sex contract. When we first got married, we were young and full of energy. We just assumed that we would always have sex every day. As the years went by, our passion slowed down. Life got in the way. We had kids and stressed about money. We had monetary obligations to our parents. Everything we encountered was new, so adjusting was always a concern. We fought a lot. We weren't having sex. It was the last thing on our minds, but it should have been the first. We went weeks without having sex, wasting time, and making things worse. I just didn't have the skillset or maturity during my younger years as a wife.

About five years ago, we decided that we needed to do something drastic, or our marriage was doomed. We came up with the sex contract—our way of defining what we sexually needed from each other. My husband confided in me that he felt deprived when we went more than four days without having some type of sexual connection—intercourse, oral sex, holding each other, or just being intimate. At that moment, I realized that we needed an intervention to prevent any further damage to our relationship. We wrote down what we needed to improve our daily lives. Sex was the common denominator. After careful deliberation, we invented our sex contract. It reads that we will never allow three days to pass without having some type of sexual interaction. This includes intercourse and oral sex. The only exception is if we are unwell or have work commitments away from home. But while away, we engage in phone sex. We must honor this contract, even during arguments. I also requested that he assist me by doing half of the household work. I needed that taken off my plate, so I didn't have to worry about it during sex. One of the reasons why I couldn't have sex in the past was because I was busy or tired. With him doing half of the chores, I have more time to spread my legs or give him a quick blow job.

The day we implemented our sex contract, our marriage changed for the better. Our sex life took a 180-degree turn, and life was full of Zen. My husband helped me with more than his share. We started doing everything together. It was as if we were learning about each other all over again, becoming true best friends. Until we implemented our sex contract, I had no idea what an impact sex had on our relationship. The greatest benefit from our contract was that we look forward to sex more than ever. Our sex got better with each encounter, instilling more positive thinking, and eliminating the negativity and white noise that previously bogged us down. The sex contract was the best thing we had ever done for our relationship. It allowed us to live in the moment and create new memories, replacing the bad ones. The sex contract enhanced our relationship exponentially. I never knew that a love like ours was possible. No one on this planet has ever loved me as much as my husband has. He's the most genuine and modest person and the hottest, kindest, and sexiest islander. He's also amazing in bed. But he can be a monster when he's mad or deprived, which is why we stay on schedule with our sex contract.

I believe a sex contract could change your relationship too. My husband and I hope to empower you to use all your available resources so you can maximize your relationship. We are giving you our hearts and souls—the good, bad, and ugly. It has been our lifelong dream to put our experiences into words. We want to reinforce your relationship the way ours was. Trust me, my husband and I are a work in progress. But by implementing a sex contract, you will spend more quality time with your partner. Most importantly, committing to your sex contract takes less energy than fighting. Don't let the ghosts of your past take control of your present. Be with your partner in the moment because it's all that we have. The toxic chaos and wasted time aren't worth it. A sex contract can assist you in deepening your love and becoming closer to your partner. It will be the best contract you have ever entered.

Without honoring our sex contract, my husband and I would not have co-written this book. I want to spend my life with my man until I take my last breath. I know that he feels the same way. It's in his every action and the way he treats me. Our book is about reinforcing relationships by being honest and transparent. Allow your partner to be their most vulnerable self. We only have one life to live. With the extremely high divorce rate, don't be a statistic. Share your true desires, wants, and needs with your partner. Compromise and establish a sex contract. With that kind of open honesty and transparency, the odds are in your favor. Know that your partner doesn't need to look elsewhere to address their needs. Satisfy each other's needs in a controlled, safe environment. Some of you are very conservative. If you would never consider experimenting, that's OK. Others may enjoy threesomes. The bottom line is you need to be honest with your partner. When you allow your other half to explore their sexuality in a safe environment, they have no reason to lie. You will lead a higher quality life without worrying that your partner may cheat or put your health at risk.

The worst part of my marriage is all the time we wasted on stupid fights. We can never get that precious time back. We could have been more productive and used it to do something beneficial, like massage each other. A massage is also one of the fastest things to arouse me. My husband and I are just like every other couple. We have our own problems, but over the years, we learned things about each other. We evolved together. If you are honest about your personal and sexual needs, you will live a higher quality life than those who are not. Many of our friends are on their second or third marriages. We want to help prevent divorce by practicing core principles that are innate in most of us. Our method isn't rocket science, and you do not have to spend any money other than the price of this book (and maybe toys or a video camera). We hope to empower all couples to become closer in intimacy and love through transparency and honesty.

I'm not a therapist, and I don't pretend to be one. I'm a mother, grandmother, and nurse who would love to bring couples closer together. I believe being married to the same man for over thirty-three years brings some validity to this book's message. My experience as a stripper gave me insight into what men want and how they think. I can empower couples to be happier and live higher-quality lives. Most of you already have what it takes to make your partner fall in love with you all over again. By the end of this book, most of you should establish a sex contract with your partner. With it, you will perform better in all areas of life.

This book won't be for everyone. Even if you disagree with our lifestyle, our message isn't meant to offend you. This book is meant to set an example for honest couples who establish a sex contract, ensuring that their sexual needs are met on a consistent basis. That, alone, will deepen any relationship and breed trust. I'm trusted because I speak and live by my truth. The bottom line is we are open, honest, and transparent with each other.

Jay: You will get plenty of sex once you get married, but it won't always work out like you assume. I was so happy that my wife and I could have some sort of understanding when it came to our sexual needs. There are so many challenges that can hinder your desires and sexual needs. In my early years, military duties took me away from my wife. I was very fortunate that I only had one lengthy assignment. We still enjoyed each other over the phone every chance we had. Our sex contract was very simple and easy. We promised to satisfy each other and have a long-lasting marriage. When we were younger, we allowed other women to come into our bedroom. But threesomes were always decisions that we both agreed on, and they took place in a controlled environment. Our experiences strengthened our marriage and made our lovemaking fulfilling.

5

Pinky

I love my husband's penis so much that I wrote a chapter to emphasize the importance of viewing your partner's penis as your personal sexual toy from a wife's perspective. I named my husband's penis Pinky because of the color—it has hues of pink and brown. Pinky is huge and rock-hard when stimulated. I feel it's important for me to have an ongoing relationship with Pinky. Like walking the dog, it must happen. Pinky needs attention, even if I am mad at my husband. The same goes for you. Even if you are mad at your partner, address your needs. And maybe give him quick blow job after you get off. View your partner's sex organ as a separate entity. This will help put things into perspective. Your man's penis controls so much of who he is and how he reacts to situations.

I have tested my husband multiple times since implementing our sex contract. When we have sex on a consistent basis, life is amazing. When my husband's cock is satisfied, everything else falls into suit. I love feeling Pinky pulsate when my husband penetrates me. I let Pinky know how much I love him. I grip him with both hands, creating a makeshift vaginal tunnel. I suck Pinky hard with deep strokes, occasionally scratching his balls until he explodes into my mouth. By making the makeshift vagina with my hands, I take some of the pressure off my jaw. After Pinky explodes, my husband can do nothing but break down and whimper while I move my hands up and down in a circular motion and suck out all of the come. Then, I scratch Pinky all over to further stimulate him. This is how I put my mark on my man. I swear he repeatedly falls in love with me from this act alone.

I always have lot of moving parts when my husband and I interact sexually. My hands are busy, as well as my mouth and tongue. We find ourselves grabbing each other's feet, holding hands, or holding each other down. It gets very passionate between us. I find it empowering to know that my mouth can take down a 260-pound Samoan in less than three minutes. Right after we make love, we hold each other. I love to listen to my husband's heartbeat until we pass out. He is defenseless against our sex, and it's all because of our sex contract. All of Pinky's wishes and desires are laid out in our sex contract.

My goal is to deplete every bit of energy he has. I do this for a few reasons: to increase his sexual endurance and to empower him to eat healthier and adhere to our workout regimen. My household runs efficiently because of the maintenance plan laid out in our sex contract. Of course, sex on its own is great, but when you couple it with being in love, it's phenomenal. A sex contract can put all your expectations on paper so that there aren't any misconceptions. No hurt feelings for either party. You can even use a calendar to check items off if that makes life easier. This will prevent your partner from pouting. My husband and I have always been deeply passionate when making love. We don't go to bed at a regular time, so our biggest issue is being tired. This is something we have been working on for years. Most mornings, I am tired and not my optimal self. I want to have the energy to perform with my husband. He deserves that for being a good, faithful partner and servant.

When I don't feel like having sex, I offer a blow job. That way his needs are addressed, and he doesn't feel resentment toward me. It is a pleasure and honor to make this man come after thirty-three years of marriage. He is my king, and he deserves the best for giving our children and me an amazing life. He is selfless and has never asked for extramarital sex or cheated on me. Things haven't always been perfect. He has lied to me on a few occasions—one of which involved him going to a strip club behind my back. It happened early on in our marriage. He went because all his friends were going, and he couldn't look like he was being controlled by his wife. He would have been viewed as less than a man. We were young and naive. Now, I realize that I shouldn't have asked him not to go. I wish we'd had a sex contract back then. I wouldn't have been lied to. That incident was an incentive for me to dance years later.

My husband also lied to me about asking the first woman that we hooked up with for another blow job. We had gone weeks without sex. Luckily for me, I had anticipated something like this happening ahead of time. I had told the woman that if my husband ever came onto her, it was a test. To this day, I don't know if she didn't give him a blow job because she didn't want to or because of what I said. I don't know if he did anything other than that. Either way, it is no big deal. We were young and freshly married.

If we'd had a sex contract, those instances might not have happened. Look at it like this, you wouldn't let your cell phone go that long without being charged, so do not let your partner go too long without connecting with you. I did and looked at what happened. My husband is not innocent, but I could have prevented those instances from happening. It is especially important to meet your partner's needs. Otherwise, they will start behaving badly. I am confident that if you develop a sex contract, everything will change in your life—literally at the cellular level. You and your partner will hold hands at the grocery store. Everything will become romantic again. This is serious business. All you must do is get intimate more often and establish a contract that you and your partner agree on. Your sex contract outlines the expectations of your relationship. Your vagina is your partner's medication, serenity, and happy place.

The other routine that I suggest you implement is scratching your partner's genitalia. This would include his balls, ball sack, and all areas around his genitals—even the hair area. Ask for a massage in return. You both need and deserve each other's touch, separate from when you are having sex. Not everything has to be about penetration. Touching each other without having sex is equally important. Provide different kinds of massages: hot stone, deep tissue, acupressure, or a simple foot massage. View your partner's genitalia as separate from their person. Consider their genitalia your sexual organ. Trust me, things will be good.

Jay: I am so happy that she loves my penis enough to name it.

6

Getting Back to the Basics

List of five things that you need in your relationship. The purpose of this is to write your needs down. You may find that you have more than five needs or less. By writing them down, they become more relevant. This list is the outline of your sex contract. You need to know what your partner's expectations are for the relationship, and they need to be clear on your needs. Time is the most precious commodity. We must not waste it on people who are not worthy of us. Here are the five thing that I need in a relationship:

1. Trust—this allows me to be my truest self and to be vulnerable. It prevents me from being riddled with anxiety when my man is out of town or far away from me.
2. Health—living a healthy lifestyle decreases my worries about getting sick. My biggest health-related fear is my family or me getting sick and not being with each other. I encourage a healthy diet and exercise. I need my partner to eat well and sustain a healthy lifestyle because

I love him and want us to be on this planet for as long as we can.

3. Honesty—this is probably the hardest attribute. I feel like it causes the most heartache and leads to a higher divorce rate. We must be able to tell our partners what we need and want. That might be a threesome, a night out at the strip club, or a hall pass. My husband thought that trust and honesty went hand in hand, but they do not. Honesty can lead to trust, but we don't trust people at first. I had to go through trials and tribulations with my husband before I could trust him.

4. Fidelity—being faithful allows me to lick, suck, and fuck without worrying about getting a disease. I have OCD, so it's vital for me to know that my husband is not cheating on me. Infidelity is one of the biggest reasons why couples break up. Go ahead, sit back and think it will not happen to you. If you get married exceedingly early in life, infidelity is almost inevitable. My husband and I got married young. We never had the chance to sew our wild oats. But we had some fun with threesomes early in our marriage. I don't regret any of it.

5. Financial security—finances are extremely painful to talk about, but they are especially important. The best way to achieve financial security is to establish and stick to a budget. Finances are a big reason why couples get divorced. When your family's financial needs are met, you reduce your risk of divorce exponentially. So watch those pennies, clip coupons, limit your time in restaurants, and make your own lunches. Trust me, no lunch tastes as good as the money it saves. Work smarter. No one wants to work forever. I hate when I see people spend eight dollars on coffee. I used to be one of them,

but not anymore. I bought a bean grinder, French press, and milk frothier. I am in love with the smell of freshly ground beans in the morning. Add some cocoa and organic, frothy milk, and I am set. If I'm feeling festive, I might sprinkle some nutmeg or cinnamon on my coffee. Coffee is a quick way to spend a lot of money fast. Watch every penny you make and save as much as you can. Stick to a reasonable budget.

Jay: I concur.

7

His Needs

I'm not going to discuss my man's needs in this chapter other than to say that they were addressed in our sex contract. Because my husband and I have been sticking to our contract (for the most part), things have been good. Instead, my focus is solely on your relationship. I want to give it the most aggressive tune-up possible and allow you and your partner to have a lifelong relationship. This is where my experience as a former stripper comes in to play. Start meeting your partner's needs now, before another person penetrates your bond. It can and will happen if his needs aren't addressed. I know my tone has changed. That's because I mean business. I want to fight for your relationship. Now is the time to take it to the next level and be as optimal as possible.

This is the most important chapter. Please read it twice. Men need as much attention as women do but on different levels. Your partner needs to be listened to and held, just like you. Not all the time, of course, but don't overlook the need for the human touch. More importantly, before your partner wants to be held, he wants to have sex—sex that is satisfying and intense. There will be many times when he will accept a blow job, but at the end of the day, he needs to come. Make it happen. Keep it moving, and your household will be Zen. Your man wants to know that he is the king of the jungle. Let him know vocally and through your actions in and out of the bed. Scratch his back and his balls as often as you can. These actions, alone, will keep him at home. When you are intimate with your man, don't hold back. Spread your legs wider, scratch him more, deep throat him deeper, and use the makeshift-vagina technique discussed in chapter 5 to take the pressure off your jaw. Be in the moment with your man.

Establish a sex contract and stick to it. Watch how it will change your relationship. Your partner needs to release his come on a regular basis, no matter what. Especially during fights. Make a journal and watch how things get better just by being in tune with his biology. He also needs to have his meals prepared. His nutrition is vital to how he acts. I suggest meal prepping. It's a task that you can do together. If you are the one working, he can prepare the meals for the most part. Ladies, take care of your men. We need to keep our men optimal so they will be on this planet for as long as possible. We look to them for everything we never got as children. We expect them to fulfill all of our needs and compensate for our deficits. We need to give back to them. This will not only make your relationship rock-solid but also do wonders for you, physically and sensually.

Clear exercise with your partner's physician. Getting in shape is necessary for life. It's important to look good for yourself first, then for your man. Exercising is more about the health benefits, especially if you suffer from anxiety. Get active in any form that you are comfortable with. Play your favorite songs, put on some sexy shoes, look in the mirror, and touch yourself all over. Fall back in love with your soul. Reinforce your chakra with mother earth. Meditate on all that you have, who you are, and who you want to become. Put it into action, and make it happen.

Your life is not just about you. It's about your legacy. That includes all of the animals in your life. They are family. Do what it takes to make yourself happy so that you can make your partner happy too. I want you to get your sexy on. With your man, go to the strip club, nude beach, nude hot springs, or somewhere else people can be their authentic selves. Let your guard down and go with the flow. Converse with others who cherish each moment in life. I'm not saying to partake in sexual interactions but learn from others who can provide good wisdom for your life.

The people who influenced me the most were those who traveled the country every chance they got. Be your truest self. Take time for yourself and your dreams. Most importantly, I want you to become a butterfly or a phoenix. Get up and live your life right now and with no regrets. The confidence is inside of you. You just need to reach down deep and make it happen. One mental decision could change your life and health and ensure a happy, healthy life with your loved one. Take care of yourself and your man. Massage each other on a regular basis. Get your self-care in. Money is the lifeline of a relationship. If you budget your money correctly, you can avoid any preventable fights. Establish a sex contract and adhere it. Make sure to look your best a few days every week to let your partner know that you still want to be sexy for him. When you are ready to take him out to a strip club, with your man. Take a nice, hot bath; wash and blow-dry your hair; lotion up; put makeup on; and wear something sexy. Grab your lipstick, ID, money, and a small purse to keep on you in case you want to have a couples' private dance. Take your partner out, and rock his world. I suggest having sex before you go. That way your man will be nice and relaxed. It is all about confidence, ladies. Let your partner know that he is your king.

I am serious. If this is the man you want to spend the rest of your life with, let him know. Do things with your man. Look at his ass. Grab his ass when you are at the gym. Whisper in his ear how fucking hot he is. Let him know that you want him to stick his penis inside of your pussy. I encourage you to have more sex with your husband, especially if you want him to do things around the house. Tell your man how sexy he is. He needs to hear it. I need to hear how sexy I am. I know, but I still want my husband to tell me. So be vocal. Don't be afraid to send your partner sexy texts. Keep the fire burning. I believe that men need to be fucked, sucked, and massaged. They need their balls scratched, healthy food to eat, a good household income, and a sex contract. That is my book in a nutshell. Men need to know that they still have it. That's a big part of their self-esteem. They feel better about themselves when they know that their women are satisfied. Don't confuse this with being pretentious and fake. It is obvious when that happens, so if your man isn't built like a stud, encourage him a little bit at a time. Compliment him the entire way. You would want the same.

Don't act like your partner's mother unless you provide total care to them, and they are not cognitively with it. Men do not like restrictions. They should know where not to go. Take your partner out to the nightclub or bar and enjoy yourselves. Make it a one-time thing if it is in your sex contract and that makes you feel better. This is all stuff that can be negotiated in your sex contract. There is nothing more natural or beautiful than women being around other beautiful women. Beauty can mean many things, and women can be beautiful in so many ways.

I encourage you to be the best version of yourself. Start right now. Live your best life, and exercise with your man. Get those endorphins pumping. Sleep well. Meet your partner's needs, and in return, he should be meeting yours. This must be equal to having a successful and happy relationship.

As I mentioned in my sex contract, I need assistance with keeping our home clean. It is very important for your partner to have a clean home. Creating a sanctuary should be your priority. A man's home is his castle and says a lot about his character. From his mother's bosom to your care. Take care of your partner in every way, and he will be happy to come home. Make it his serene sanctuary: a place he wants to spend all his time when he is not at work or doing something that he enjoys. The basics are food and shelter. Make a crockpot meal, and keep the home clean and comfy, no matter where you live. Make it homey and personal. Make a space in the living room that is just his—maybe a little table with a glass of water so he and his sexual organ can stay hydrated. Make sure he has a place designated for him. Be your husband's biggest advocate. Make sure that he is eating healthy, and he will know how much you care. You can make an occasional cheat meal for him, like biscuits and gravy. Send your partner romantic or sexual texts. Leave him notes to say that you can't wait for him to be inside of you again. Don't forget to remind him how beautiful his muscles are, even if he is a little undesirable. Encourage your man to continue going to the gym. Don't go overboard. Don't be fake. Just be real. You want your man to be the best version of himself, both mentally and physically. Again, make sure that you are cooking balanced meals and giving him snacks in moderation. These are just options so that he can perform better in bed.

I also recommend playing music that you guys like. Dance to the songs you listened to when you were dating. Listen to the songs that make you want to exercise and move so that you both can get into shape. Take videos of you and your husband when you are intimate to watch later or when you are apart from each other. Capture your moments and techniques to reflect on and enjoy later. Your man has needs that must be addressed, no matter what you have going on in your life. He doesn't care that you have kids to take care of. He loves you and his kids but feels that it's up to you to prioritize your time. He, in return, should assist you in any way he can. This includes doing 50 percent of all the childcare and housework. Or whatever the needs of your household may be. If you are tired or overwhelmed, you cannot be expected to fulfill someone else's needs. In those times, the sex contract is vital. It takes the pressure away and can equally divide the chores.

Jay: I have no doubt that my wife holds my best interests at heart. She will always consider my thoughts when choosing how to live with me. I've never wanted or needed my own space. We kind of mutually agree on certain things that I like to do (such as golf), so I have time to enjoy life outside of the home. I've never had the urge to explore the nightlife or life away from the home. I don't ask for much, and in return, I never expect anything more than everyday life with my wife since the kids have grown up and moved out. My sanctuary is the idea that I'm making her happy. My needs have always been very simple—I need sex every day and to live life like it's the last day. That doesn't mean everything is simple. Marriage and kids can be complicated. I'm talking about only the simple little things. If my wife and I are having a wonderful day, I won't start something minute that could ruin life's precious minutes.

Instead of arguing over something so unnecessary, just drop it or keep it closed. My need outside of playing golf is my wife. For our marriage to be a success, we can't afford to waste time on the unnecessary sidetracks that cause undue stress and misery.

8

Your Needs

My needs are simple. I need to be loved, satisfied, honored, respected, protected, and financially stable. I want my husband to spend the rest of his life being faithful to me. I want us to be together until we take our last breaths and to spend all of my time with my family. I want my family to have a lifetime of health, wealth, and longevity. I want to travel the world. I want to stick to the sex contract that my husband and I established and ensure a Zen household. I want you and every person that reads my message to know that it comes from a sincere, genuine place. Live your best life, and let no one stand in your way, including you. Be as honest, open, and transparent about your needs as possible to live the highest quality of life with your partner.

What are your needs? I encourage you to do some deep soul-searching to determine how you want to live the rest of your life. Articulate these wants and needs to your partner. It's so refreshing to be in a relationship that is honest, transparent, and safe. I am a highly anxious, type-A person. My husband calms me by always recognizing when I am anxious. He will have me breathe. He may meditate with me in that moment to slow my heart rate. He protects me by intervening and deflating the situation. He is my natural Xanax, and sex with him is my vitamin. I just want to give back for all the things he has done for me. Our marriage is not always great. It takes work. Sometimes things get in the way, like our pride or need to be right. Sometimes we can't even recognize the useless time and energy we waste by fighting. It is infuriating when we look back at the time we have wasted. As a nurse, I know better than to take life for granted, but I still get caught up in the littlest of things at times, taking me away from my husband and our time together.

Please don't waste any more precious time. You cannot get it back. None of us has any time to waste. The focus should be on creating more good memories and fading out the bad to the best of our abilities. Do not waste one more second on stupid shit. Whatever you are doing right now, let it be for the betterment of yourself and your relationship. Get up, put on some stilettos and a negligée, and start stripping in your bedroom right now. Start a new workout regimen and execute it. Work out with your man in your living room at home. Let him know that you notice and appreciate his body and want to take care of it. Food prep with him. Make him want to marry you all over again. Make him so excited to see you that he rushes home every day. Take him out to the strip club. Embrace being around other beautiful women. You can appreciate the beauty and youth of another woman without doubting your unique gorgeousness.

Embrace your femininity. Soak in the tub longer. Leave your hair up. Take better care of yourself. Be your most beautiful and confident self. Let others know how much respect and love you have for yourself and your partner. I am asking you to change your energy into something productive for your marriage. It can be whatever you need it to be. Take care of your partner so they can receive your message and fulfill your needs. For example, when your man is sexually satisfied, he will do whatever you want, usually without having to be asked. He will cook, clean, run errands, and show how much he cares by being available any time. He will give you access to anything that you desire.

Another amazing way to provide yourself with optimal self-care is to masturbate. I think that women should do it for mental maintenance every other day if they are not able to have sex with their spouses. Or maybe they did and didn't come. You can always masturbate. I masturbate through my clothes while in a prone position. I have never penetrated myself to have an orgasm. I can simply straddle my own fingers near my clitoris and ride them until I orgasm. I hardly ever masturbate, but when I do, that is how I roll. It's such an amazing relief. It's extremely healthy and increases my endorphins. For the most part, I masturbate while thinking of my husband with another woman. That is me being honest and transparent with all of you. There are times when my husband and I make love and I still want more. When that happens, I flip over onto my husband's hand and ride his finger until I explode.

Another very important reason to masturbate is to relieve nausea. It works wonders. If you are experiencing stress and your partner is not around, I recommend masturbating for quick relief. I personally masturbated for a year while my husband was overseas. We had a lot of phone sex, as it was before social media.

If you are not really in the mood and need to speed up your sexual experience, go ahead and implement the art of faking. I do it about one out of every ten times and only because I am ready to go to sleep. Once I get my orgasm, it's time to get him to his happy ending. I know my husband so well that there is a point in our lovemaking that if I just pretend, he will explode. He is very much aware that I do fake it sometimes. To be honest, he is very much okay with it.

So, put my book down. Put it down! Look in the mirror and tell yourself that you are worth it. When you wake up in the morning (after you have peed), jump on your scale and weigh yourself. Write your weight down. This is your starting point. It will only get better from here. Before you go on a diet, discuss it with your physician. I recommend playing your favorite tune on your Bluetooth and jamming out as soon as you get of out of bed. If you need to drink your coffee first, go for it, but then get right back to some physical fitness. I also suggest drinking lemon water if your doctor approves. And start working on your mental and physical well-being. Avoid all processed foods and eat whole foods. When you're in shape, you feel good. So, keep working out, and keep those endorphins pumping. Ensure that you are getting eight hours of sleep. Stay hydrated and eat a balanced diet. You must be 100 percent for your VIP—you!

Jay: For over thirty-three years, I have always tried to meet my wife's needs. She is a complicated woman because of her OCD. I've learned to be patient and try to look at things from her perspective. But it's very, very challenging at times. Sometimes I don't meet her needs, and that's disappointing. But one thing is for sure—I can satisfy her every need when it comes to intimacy. Whether it's a quick fuck or just performing oral on her, I do it at 100 percent. I take pride in satisfying her in that way. I would feel like a failure if I didn't perform. We wasted so much time because one of us didn't compromise with the other. I was never a romantic person, but she was. I had to work hard to meet her halfway. I was also very stubborn because I didn't like to repeat myself. My wife was always looking for affirmation or confirmation of my love. I've grown to accommodate her through the years, and it has made life so much easier, resulting in happiness.

9

Execution and Delivery

When you and your partner are ready to establish your sex contract, make sure you are both aware that this should be taken seriously for the betterment of your relationship. Hold your sex contract in the same regard as your marriage contract. Fights are temporary, but your marriage is forever. My recommendation is that you always honor your sex contract.

The first thing you need to do is come up with a game plan for yourself and your relationship. Start this very moment by caring for yourself. It won't hurt you to take ten extra minutes to floss and brush your teeth and apply lotion to your entire body. Apply some mascara and a light coat of lipstick—nothing too much; this isn't your new normal. Throw your hair up into a ponytail or messy bun and exude sexiness because that's exactly what you are. After clearing your exercise routine with your doctor, work out to your favorite jams in the morning to sweat and get your heart rate up. Eat right. Get the stripper mentality: look sexy by wearing sexy clothes and shoes. Take pride in your looks! Rock it and remember that anyone can be sexy and confident if they are healthy. It doesn't matter who you are. If you are the best version of yourself and exude confidence, you are sexy. I want you to love yourselves fiercely so that others will know exactly how to treat you. Be the best role model for your partner, children, and every other person that comes into your life by being a happy, productive individual.

We only have one life. We should be happy and do things to extend life to the fullest. We all have different needs and must work hard to ensure they are fulfilled. Life is too short not to experience new things with your partner. By being brutally honest about yours and your partner's needs, you create an environment that your partner will be drawn to and will want to come home to every night. No one needs to hide or sneak around. You will be able to share most things with your partner that you could share with your friends. I want to empower you to find a middle ground and satisfy the needs of your relationship. You can have the relationship that all your friends strive for but don't have. All you must do is trust your partner and work with them toward the same goals. By establishing and sticking to your sex contract, life will start to become a lot simpler. You and your partner will never have to worry about outside influences. In these days and times, cheating is too easy, especially with all the new secretive ways like swiping left on phone apps, legal prostitution, or colleagues at the office. It can all be prevented.

I want you to create and control your own environment, ensuring the highest quality of life possible. You don't have to spend any money or attend a class. Most of you already possess the skillsets you need. Just be honest and allow your partner to be honest with you in a safe, calm environment without judgment. If you don't allow this, cheating will happen, and it won't be in a controlled environment. As far-fetched as it seems to be honest about your sexual needs, the ability to do so plants a seed of trust that can only come from brutally honesty. Meeting your partner's needs will lead to a lifetime of faithful happiness. You can establish your own definition of faithfulness. Our definition means honesty, transparency, and all sexual activity happening in front of each other. I want everyone to feel that they are "the couple." I am talking about being "that couple," "couple goals," or true soulmates.

I am confident that my experiences after thirty-three years of marriage and as a former stripper can help all of you, as it has helped my husband and me. We hold hands almost everywhere we go. I still get butterflies when I see him. I am confident that I can impact your life and improve the quality of your marriage. I have the necessary tools to empower you to make positive changes and ensure a lifetime of happiness. They will also give you the confidence to know that your partner would pick you all over again. I hope that you will love yourself like no other, be patient, teach your partner what you need, and allow them to grow into the best version of themselves. This book has a lot to do with sex because sex is our lifeline—our battery charger if you will. It's what connects us to our partners and is especially important for any relationship. Through my experiences as a stripper and with pain and wasted time, I know that if I had taken my advice and kept my husband sexually satisfied, most of what we argued about would have never existed. Please learn from me. Take a little piece of my life experience and use it as a reference for yours.

At the end of the day, any positive change that you implement into your marriage can have a ripple effect, changing everything else. Wouldn't you rather use that energy on massaging each other, slow dancing to whatever random song comes on, or working out together? Me too. It took me a long time to realize that simply giving a blow job, a quick screw, or making love would keep my man on even keel for a couple of days. Win the war; don't waste time on the battle. I am giving you 100 percent of the most intimate parts of our lives together. The reason I am sharing this story is so you will be honest and transparent about your needs, allowing you to have the best relationship possible. I feel that by being honest and transparent, you will be able to live your best life. You have everything you need to maximize your relationships. Share your true desires, wants, and needs with your spouse. Compromise. With that kind of open honesty and transparency, a lifelong relationship is possible.

Jay: I concur.

10

A How-to Guide on Establishing a Sex Contract

1. Do some deep soul searching to ascertain your needs and desires—things that you are uncomfortable with versus things forbidden in your sex contract.
2. Find the person who is worthy of establishing a sex contract with and make the commitment. Go to the nearest health clinic or your personal physician, and have blood drawn to determine if there are any sexually transmitted diseases. Run a background check. If both areas check out, establish a sex contract.
3. Get a piece of notebook paper or create a spreadsheet. Start your budget. You can't lay in bed and have sex if you don't have a job. No one wants a broke partner. Come up with a budget that will allow you to pay your bills and save money. Money is a big stressor in marriage and a big reason for divorce.
4. Write down your sex contract, or verbally come to an agreement so long as your requests aren't too long or hard

to remember. Include rules of engagement. One of our rules is that we will continue to have sex, even when we are upset. We may not want to make love, but we must at least have sex. Oral is normally all I give when I'm upset or tired. He always wants it all, but that was not in our contract. Even though I love giving it all to him, I am tired and busy. Sometimes, I just need to get it knocked out.

5. Execute your sex contract to achieve the highest quality of life as possible. This will not only reinforce your bond with the one you love but also prevent any unnecessary tension that would exacerbate everyday problems.

Jay: I concur.

Our Sex Contract

Intercourse and/or oral sex every *two to three days* if not sooner unless we are *busy or unwell*. Domestic obligations should be *split in half*, 50 percent.

That is the extent of our sex contract. It's equal for both of us across the board. Chores are a big responsibility and should not fall on one person. It is especially important to me that he assist with the domestic needs of the household. If he didn't, I wouldn't be able to meet the expectations of my relationship. I assist him with the outdoor tasks as well. The rules must always be consistent and fair.

Now that you know how to establish your own sex contract, you can get to work! You don't have to go out and buy anything. Just schedule some time with your partner that will allow you to discuss both of your needs freely. Then jot down your wants and needs. Compromise and negotiate, and in the end, you will establish a sex contract that will work for both of you. It's as easy as that. I promise you that this will be the best contract you have ever stuck to. Your partner will always have their needs addressed, preventing (if not eliminating) any unnecessary tension in your relationship.

Conclusion

Thank you so much for reading our book. We hope it reinforces your relationship like ours has been. Your sex contract will afford you and your partner quality time together. Most importantly, committing to your sex contract will take less energy than fighting. Do not let the ghosts of your past take control of your present. Be with your partner in this moment, as it's all that we have. The toxic chaos and wasted time are not worth it. A sex contract can and will make all the difference when implemented in a loving, respectful relationship. But it won't work by itself. You must be committed to the work.

You and your partner will establish the contents of your sex contract. It will deepen your love. You will be so close that you won't know where they end, and you begin. Go and put on their sexy, white business shirt; play the song you both love, and let biology happen. Reward your faithful servant for their faithful service. Make sure you sexually deplete them, conquering them until all they can do is whimper. Let your partner know how worthy they is, and they will show you how worthy you are.

Remember to take care of yourself from the inside, out. Be the sexiest version of yourself. Keep the home fires burning because your relationship should be your priority. Sex contracts apply to all couples in loving relationships or marriages. There is no better time than now to learn new tools and improve the most important relationships in our lives. Get on a path to understand yourself. Enrich your and your partner's lives. Be good role models to your children and everyone that you encounter. Make the planet a better place. Give someone hope by being a good human.